THE SUN & MOON SIGNS LIBRARY

GEMINI

MAY 22 – JUNE 21

JULIA AND DEREK PARKER

Photography by Monique le Luhandre
Illustrations by Danuta Mayer

Dedicated to Peter Heggie

A DK PUBLISHING BOOK

Editor **Tom Fraser**
Art Editor **Ursula Dawson**
Managing Editor **Krystyna Mayer**
Managing Art Editor **Derek Coombes**
Production **Antony Heller**
U.S. Editor **Laaren Brown**

Computer page make-up Patrizio Semproni.
Photography p 10 Museum of Antiquities, Newcastle Upon Tyne/ Bridgeman
Art Library, London; p 11 Ronald Sheridan/Ancient Art and Architecture Collection;
p 16 Tim Ridley. Stylist pp 28-29 Lucy Elworthy. Illustration
pp 60-61 Kuo Kang Chen. Jacket illustration Peter Lawman.
With thanks to Carolyn Lancaster and John Filbey.

First American Edition, 1992
10 9 8 7 6 5

Published in the United States by
DK Publishing, Inc., 95 Madison Avenue,
New York, N.Y. 1006

Visit us on the World Wide Web at
http://www.dk.com

Library of Congress Catalog Card Number 92-52786
ISBN 1-56458-086-5

Reproduced by GRB Editrice, Verona, Italy

Printed and bound in India

CONTENTS

INTRODUCING
GEMINI

GEMINI, THE SIGN OF THE HEAVENLY TWINS, IS THE THIRD
ZODIAC SIGN. GEMINIAN SUBJECTS ARE NOTED FOR
THEIR DUALITY: THEY SELDOM RESTRICT THEMSELVES
TO DOING JUST ONE THING AT A TIME.

Being the first sign of the air element, Gemini bestows a light intellect. This is reflected in the fact that Geminians tend to know a little about a great range of subjects. Geminians must be aware that superficiality can lead to shallowness of character, and that restlessness may prevent them from ever managing to achieve their full potential. While recognizing that variety is essential for them, Geminians must try to develop continuity of effort if they are to achieve inner fulfillment.

Traditional groupings

As you read through this book you will come across references to the elements and the qualities, and to positive and negative, or masculine and feminine signs.

The first of these groupings, that of the elements, comprises fire, earth, air, and water signs. The second, that of the qualities, divides the Zodiac

into cardinal, fixed, and mutable signs. The final grouping is made up of positive and negative, or masculine and feminine signs. Each Zodiac sign is associated with a combination of components from these groupings, all of which contribute different characteristics to it.

Geminian characteristics

The Geminian ruling planet is Mercury, which often inclines its subjects to be good communicators. Gemini is also of the mutable quality, which heightens the properties of Mercury and the intellectual approach characteristic of the sign itself.

Gemini is a positive, masculine sign, and is regarded as the most youthful of all the 12 signs of the Zodiac. Although many different colors will no doubt appeal to individual Geminians, there is, overall, a tendency for them to favor shades of yellow.

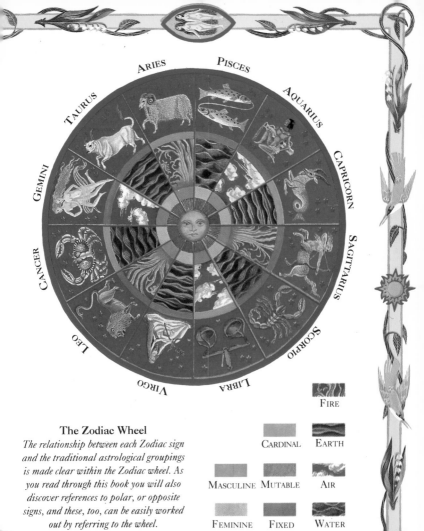

ARIES PISCES

TAURUS AQUARIUS

GEMINI CAPRICORN

CANCER SAGITTARIUS

LEO SCORPIO

VIRGO LIBRA

FIRE

CARDINAL EARTH

MASCULINE MUTABLE AIR

FEMININE FIXED WATER

The Zodiac Wheel

*The relationship between each Zodiac sign
and the traditional astrological groupings
is made clear within the Zodiac wheel. As
you read through this book you will also
discover references to polar, or opposite
signs, and these, too, can be easily worked
out by referring to the wheel.*

MYTHS & LEGENDS

THE ZODIAC, WHICH IS SAID TO HAVE ORIGINATED IN
BABYLON AS LONG AS 2,500 YEARS AGO, IS A
CIRCLE OF CONSTELLATIONS THROUGH WHICH THE SUN
MOVES DURING THE COURSE OF A YEAR.

Gemini is one of only two signs whose myth has some pictorial connection with the pattern of stars that make up its constellation: it was so called because of the two bright stars it contains. The Babylonians called it the Great Twins in their Zodiac. The myth most strongly associated with the sign is that of Castor and Pollux, known as the Dioscuri, which means "the young sons of Zeus." The paternity of Castor and Pollux is in fact a complicated affair. While their mortal parents were Leda and Tyndareus, a union between Zeus, the king of the gods, disguised as a swan, and Leda confuses the issue. Leda produced two eggs. From one came Pollux and Helen; from the other, Castor and Clytemnestra. Pollux and Helen (later to be known as Helen of Troy) were said to be the children of Zeus, and therefore immortal, whereas Castor and Clytemnestra were assumed to be the mortal children of Tyndareus. It was in fact quite common for people of ancient civilizations to claim that one child from a pair of twins was

Helmet cheekpiece
*A typical Roman image
of one of the Dioscuri.*

of divine origin. Castor and Pollux were brought up in Sparta, where they formed a very close friendship.

Among their exploits together, Castor and Pollux rescued their sister, Helen, from an abductor, Theseus, and joined Jason and the Argonauts' expedition to recover the Golden Fleece. Afterward the two boys fell in love with two sisters, Hilaeira and Phoebe, who were already betrothed at the time. When the boys carried them off, Castor was tragically killed in the ensuing brawl. Pollux, the immortal, could not bear the thought of being parted from his brother and wept over his body. Touched by the sight of such brotherly devotion, Zeus allowed Pollux to share his immortality with Castor. As a result, the twins spent half their time in the Underworld with the spirits of the dead, and half with the gods on Mount Olympus.

Great athletes when on Earth, Castor and Pollux became patrons of all athletic contests. They were also said to protect sailors, to whom they still appear during storms as the lights of St. Elmo's fire. This belief dates back to the occasion when Zeus saved the Argonauts from a violent storm that was threatening to sink their ship, the Argo: Two flames came down from the heavens and hung above the heads of the Dioscuri, signaling the end of the storm. In later times, Castor and Pollux were regarded as divine and, according to legend, were supposed to ride through the sky on two white horses, carrying dazzling spears, each with a star above his brow. During the years of Imperial Rome, Castor and Pollux were believed to descend to Earth in order to fight at the head of the Roman army whenever it did battle with its enemies.

People who have a Geminian Sun sign tend to possess two distinct sides to their natures, enabling them to do two things at once. Duality is therefore very likely to constitute a strong part of your personality.

Roman Republican coin
This coin from 210 B.C. shows Castor and Pollux riding through the heavens.

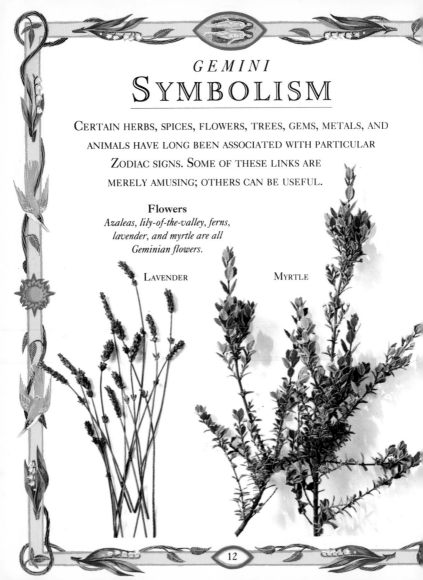

GEMINI
SYMBOLISM

CERTAIN HERBS, SPICES, FLOWERS, TREES, GEMS, METALS, AND
ANIMALS HAVE LONG BEEN ASSOCIATED WITH PARTICULAR
ZODIAC SIGNS. SOME OF THESE LINKS ARE
MERELY AMUSING; OTHERS CAN BE USEFUL.

Flowers
*Azaleas, lily-of-the-valley, ferns,
lavender, and myrtle are all
Geminian flowers.*

LAVENDER

MYRTLE

Trees
All nut-bearing trees are ruled by Gemini, but especially the hazel and walnut.

ANISEED

Spices
No spices are particularly associated with Gemini, but many people of this sign tend to enjoy spicy food, perhaps seasoned with aniseed or caraway.

HAZEL

CARAWAY

Herbs
Lemon balm is good for curing a stitch, and arrowroot can be applied to a blister. An infusion of nettles soothes a sore throat. All of these herbs are governed by Gemini.

LEMON BALM

GEMINI
SYMBOLISM

MERCURY

Metal
*Mercury is both the Geminian
ruling planet and, as its
popular name, quicksilver,
suggests, the Geminian metal.*

AGATE

INDIAN PARROT SPICE BOX

Gems
*Agates and emeralds are
Geminian stones. But
Geminians like all colors, so
most glittering gems will
appeal to them.*

WOODEN BIRD BROOCH

1920s CRÊPE PAPER
BUTTERFLY FAN

BUTTERFLY BROOCH

Animals

*The chattering monkey is
certainly a Geminian beast, and
so, traditionally, are small,
swift, brightly colored birds
and butterflies.*

CHINA MONKEY

BRASS MONKEYS

GEMINI
PROFILE

THE OVERALL APPEARANCE OF A GEMINIAN IS USUALLY LIVELY,
OFTEN REFLECTING RESTLESSNESS AND A KEENNESS TO BE
UP TO THE MINUTE. GEMINIANS ARE OFTEN RECOGNIZED BY
THEIR SPRIGHTLY, LIGHT-FOOTED WAY OF WALKING.

Geminians seem to hardly ever stand still. In a queue at a drinks party you will, for example, spend most of your time moving restlessly up and down, on and off the balls of your feet.

The body

The Geminian body is usually long and lean. Because you have a fast metabolism, you are not inclined to put on weight; so if you are tall and slender, the chances are that you will stay that way for the whole of your life. Your arms and legs may be long, and your hands prominent and flexible. Some Geminians give the appearance of being a little bony. Geminian shoulders are not wide, and may tend

The Geminian face
You may have lively-looking features, and short, cropped hair.

to slope a little. It is very important for you to keep moving in order to burn up your high level of tense, physical Geminian energy.

The face

Many Geminians have fine hair that is cropped into an easily manageable style. Your forehead could well be rather broad, which will make you appear intelligent, and your eyes will be extremely alert, giving your whole face mobility and a bright expression. It is generally said that Geminians never stop talking, and it may well be the case with you that your lips do not seem to stop moving. You are also likely to have a particularly attractive mouth. The Geminian chin is

The Geminian stance
Many Geminians have a tendency to bob up and down on the balls of their feet whenever they have to wait for anything.

typically sharp, and sometimes pointed, which adds to the overall lively appearance.

Style
Geminians are fashionable, and like to wear the very latest styles – often favoring separates. Sometimes, through your need for variety, a "mix and match" policy may not pay off, and your appearance could become haphazard. However, with a little experience most Geminians can develop the gift of mixing separates in clever and interesting ways.

Accessories are very popular among Geminians, with trendy hats, sunglasses, belts, and fashion jewelry generally much in evidence. You may manage to accumulate quite a collection of these things. Most colors are popular among Geminians, but yellow particularly so.

In general
Even if you do not possess the typical Geminian physique, it is probable that you will still be be immediately recognizable, even from a distance,

because of your distinctive way of walking: Geminians seem to positively bob up and down, as much as they move forward.

Irrespective of your nationality, you probably gesticulate with your hands and arms more than people of other Sun signs. Every movement that you make is likely to be quick, rather sudden, and sometimes even a little twitchy or jerky.

17

PERSONALITY

GEMINIANS POSSESS NIMBLE MINDS AND BODIES. THE TWINS,
WHICH SYMBOLIZE THE SIGN, REPRESENT THE
GEMINIAN NEED TO BE ACTIVE IN A NUMBER OF DIFFERENT
FIELDS AT THE SAME TIME.

Simply because it is not in your nature, it would be wrong to urge you to do just one thing at a time. The rest of us must, however, see to it that in due course you get around to completing each project you start. This will probably subdue any restlessness and help you to achieve a sense of inner satisfaction.

At work

Geminians tend to function at a high level of nervous tension. If this is expressed positively, through work that you find rewarding, it will be burned off in a satisfactory way. On the other hand, if you are involved in repetitive work or are forced to tolerate stupidity, a great deal of stress can build up. In such cases it is very important that you find ways to ease the tension. A boring or undemanding job should be balanced with some stimulating continuing education courses. Alternatively, an exacting

intellectual job should perhaps be tempered by some form of lively competitive leisure activity, such as tennis or squash.

Geminians know a little about a lot of different subjects, and are often quite rightly accused of being superficial. This could be a difficult hurdle for you to overcome, although one way might be to develop variety within the confines of a few well-chosen subjects. This will ensure that your notoriously low threshold of boredom is not reached.

Your attitudes

You possess great cunning, and because you are recognized to be the communicators of the Zodiac, you will have no difficulty in expressing ideas and opinions to anyone who cares to listen. In doing so, you will manage to change people's ideas and opinions to match your own way of thinking. This will often be accomplished very

Mercury rules Gemini
*Mercury, the messenger god, represents the ruling planet of
Gemini. The influence of Mercury stimulates the mind, but it
can also make its subjects critical, nervous, and tense.*

artfully, without people realizing that you are doing it. Be careful, however, that your native cunning does not involve duplicity.

The overall picture

It must be remembered that the Geminian mind needs continual stimulation, and the Geminian body continual movement. Both physical and mental energy must be regulated like a well-oiled machine and released at a constant level.

Geminians are usually highly motivated and can end up being great achievers, especially if they are involved in the media or sales. The influence of your ruling planet, Mercury, will help you, since Mercury is the messenger god.

GEMINI
ASPIRATIONS

IDEALLY, GEMINI WOULD LIKE TO HAVE A NEW JOB EVERY DAY.
THE CHANCES ARE THAT A REGULAR ROUTINE WILL
BORE YOU STIFF. IF YOU DO HAVE TO PUT UP WITH ONE, A
VARIETY OF SPARE-TIME ACTIVITIES IS ESSENTIAL.

1920s OFFICE
INTERCOM
SYSTEM

Reception work
*Geminians usually
prosper in jobs related to
communications. This is
due to an association with
the planet Mercury,
which is linked
with activity.*

Teaching
*Geminians are not
known for their patience,
so if they become teachers –
a good choice given their
excellent communications
skills – they should
choose to
work with
older children
or teenagers.*

PENCIL SET

1920s
TELEPHONE
EXTENSION

OLD BANK NOTES

International banking
The wheeling and dealing and intense activity of either international banking or a stock exchange will suit many Geminians.

Telecommunications
This type of work will suit those who are fond of communication, especially conversation.

TOOLS USED IN
GRAPHIC DESIGN

MINIATURE CASH REGISTER

Media work
Many Geminians work in the media. This includes graphic design, public relations, and publicity.

Retail sales
Many Geminians have the ability to get along with anyone and to sell anything. You might enjoy the busy, lively atmosphere of a large department store.

21

HEALTH

GEMINI IS AN AIR SIGN, AND THIS INFLUENCES THE LUNGS.
FOR GEMINIANS LIVING IN AN UNPOLLUTED
ENVIRONMENT IS CRITICAL. THE ARMS AND HANDS
ARE ALSO VULNERABLE.

Geminians are usually fortunate enough to have a fast metabolic rate and are unlikely to put on weight. They have the reputation of being the most youthful of all the signs, never seeming to get old.

Your diet

The Geminian diet should be light, with plenty of fresh fruit and vegetables. You may need to supplement your diet with kali muriaticum (kali. mur.), which is essential for the formation of fibron. This will help prevent bronchial congestion and swollen glands.

Taking care

Gemini rules the lungs, and there is no doubt that Geminians can suffer from bad coughs. Remember that negligence may seriously weaken your lungs. You should also try not to smoke; the habit could prove to be even more dangerous for you than it is for other people.

Gemini partly rules the shoulders and many Geminians fracture collar bones, often while participating in a sport. The Geminian hands and arms are also extremely vulnerable; you may get a lot of cuts and splinters.

Walnuts

Most nuts, and many vegetables grown above ground, are traditionally regarded as Geminian foods.

Astrology and the body

For many centuries it was not possible to practice medicine without a knowledge of astrology. In European universities, medical training included information on how planetary positions would affect the administration of medicines, the bleeding of patients, and the right time to pick herbs and make potions. Each Zodiac sign rules a particular part of the body – from Aries (the head) to Pisces (the feet) – and textbooks always included a drawing of a "Zodiac man" (or woman) that illustrated the point.

GEMINI AT
LEISURE

THE SUN SIGNS TRADITIONALLY SUGGEST SPARE-TIME ACTIVITIES,
HOBBIES, AND VACATION SPOTS. YOU SHOULD CONSIDER
SOME OF THESE SUGGESTIONS – THEY OFTEN SUIT GEMINIAN
TASTES AND INTERESTS.

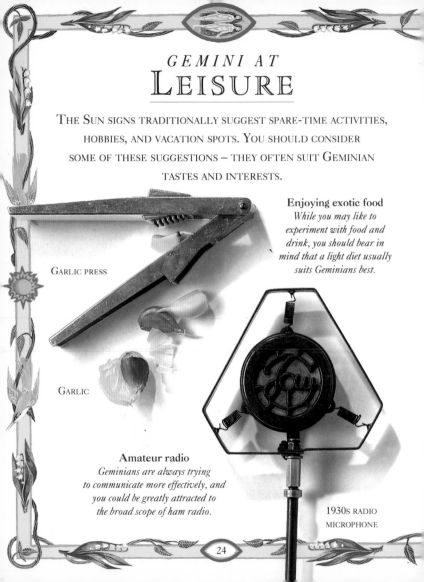

GARLIC PRESS

GARLIC

Enjoying exotic food
*While you may like to
experiment with food and
drink, you should bear in
mind that a light diet usually
suits Geminians best.*

Amateur radio
*Geminians are always trying
to communicate more effectively, and
you could be greatly attracted to
the broad scope of ham radio.*

1930S RADIO
MICROPHONE

Massage

Geminians are traditionally very sensitive, so you may be attracted to massage. It is often used as a sensual means of expression between lovers.

Massage oils

Postage stamps

Travel

Whichever destination you choose (and the United States, Belgium, Egypt, and Wales are all associated with Gemini) your main concern will be to get there quickly, so that you can enjoy yourself.

Sewing pins

Dressmaking scissors

Dressmaking

While many Geminians enjoy dressmaking, they do usually need quick results: "Make it tonight, wear it tomorrow" is usually their motto.

Tailor's chalk

GEMINI IN
LOVE

WHEN GEMINI REALIZES THAT CUPID'S DART HAS HIT HOME,
A CAMPAIGN TO ATTRACT THE ATTENTION OF THE
ADMIRED ONE WILL IMMEDIATELY BE LAUNCHED. WHAT IS
MORE, THIS PLAN USUALLY WORKS.

You may not exactly overwhelm your lovers with passion early in an affair. However, they will no doubt enjoy themselves.

People with a Gemini Sun sign wallow in the exciting period when friendship is turning to love, and will often try to draw it out. In all Geminian relationships there are strong ties of friendship and intellectual rapport. Geminians are always happy to sing praises or indulge in a little flattery, so your lovers will always know where they stand. You will usually follow up a first flirtation with a suggestion for a date, and the occasion will never be dull or ordinary. You may decide on a rock concert or a picnic in the park.

As a lover
This sign is not as highly charged, emotionally, as some others, but Geminians enjoy a lively and very varied sex life. There is a vivacious freshness in their lovemaking, even if there is as strong a need for friendship as for passion. Despite what has been said, Geminians usually have what it takes to keep a relationship alive and flourishing. If a partner responds well to new developments and

changes within the relationship, everything should proceed smoothly. You will eventually develop constancy in love, but because of the low boredom threshold of all Geminians, you will have to think hard about this before making a final commitment. It can be all too easy for you to get bored with a relationship, and for restlessness to result in considerable unhappiness.

Types of Geminian lover
Some Geminians are demonstrative and passionate, but can express an element of selfishness in their relationships. While they are warm and sexy, they must learn to consider their partner's needs. Others, while being extremely affectionate and demanding an element of independence within a relationship, can turn out to be very possessive. A third type of Geminian will have a beautifully calm and tender side in the way they express love, and will be real romantics. Other people of this Sun sign like to show off. They can be generous to a fault, but may tend to overdramatize minor upsets. This type of Geminian is very easily hurt by even the most minor upsets in a relationship.

GEMINI AT
HOME

PLENTY OF LIGHT, A PLETHORA OF GADGETS, AND THE LATEST
DESIGN FEATURES CHARACTERIZE THE TYPICAL GEMINIAN
HOME. THE COLORS ARE BRIGHT, AND THERE IS A VARIETY OF
PATTERNS IN THE WALLPAPER AND CURTAINS.

Simple, uncluttered lines dominate the Geminian home, and yellow is often a favorite color choice for walls and furnishings. Glass and shiny chrome plate is popular among people of this sign, and may be combined to make a handsome dining table. As a Sun sign Geminian, you are likely to aim for an overall lightness in your decoration schemes.

Furniture

Most Geminians like to be up to date, and therefore choose the very latest styles of furniture for their homes. Your inner restlessness can, however, sometimes cause you to become dissatisfied with what you choose. After a year or two, you probably feel the need to acquire something newer and more fashionable.

Soft furnishings

You probably like to keep soft furnishings to a minimum, placing no great emphasis on heavy drapes. If you use cushions, they will be original

Workstation

A hectic workstation, with a telephone, notepads, and a fax machine, is likely to be a feature in any Geminian home.

Personal stereo and headphones
A love of gadgets is a typically Geminian trait. People of this Sun sign also enjoy loud music.

in design, and somewhat unusual in style. Lightweight blinds, as an alternative to drapes, are popular among Geminians. Since Gemini is an air sign, your choice of furnishing fabrics or rugs never provokes a feeling of claustrophobia.

Decorative objects

It is in the choice of objects that Geminians usually display most of their lively personality traits. Being the arch communicators of the Zodiac, Geminians usually place their telephones in prominent positions.

You probably possess a great many magazines on an equally wide range of subjects. This underlines your Geminian versatility, and a general desire to keep up with what is going on. Records and cassettes, and the means to play them, are in evidence, as is no doubt a good video recorder and possibly a camera. Your ideal choice of painting could be something fairly enigmatic; perhaps a print of a Kandinsky, Dufy, or a Klee – unless you are lucky enough to be able to afford the real thing. A picture by one of these artists, or similarly minded lesser-known painters, will leave you with enough space to come to your own conclusions about the artist's original intentions and then, perhaps after a while, to rethink your ideas again.

Delicate, bright fabric
A Geminian home will be incomplete without some light, bright fabrics.

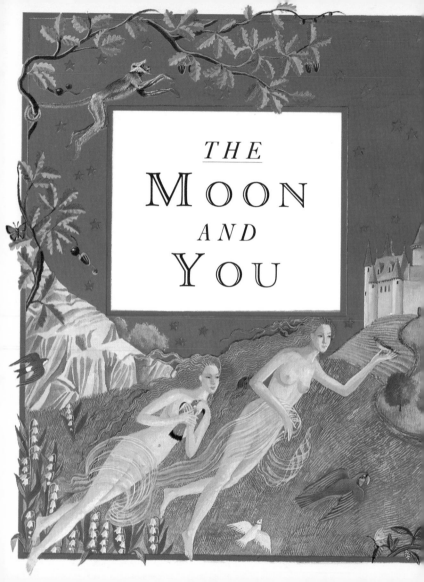

THE
MOON
AND
YOU

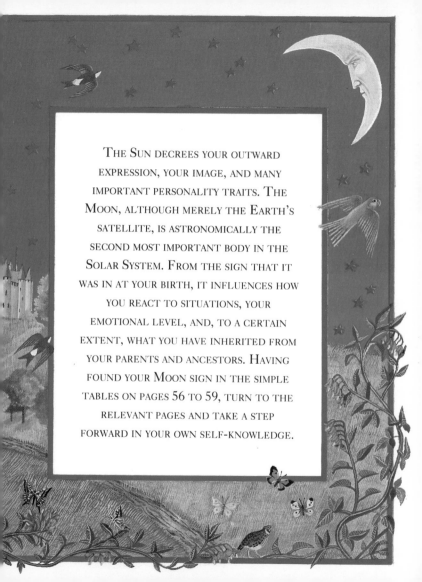

THE SUN DECREES YOUR OUTWARD
EXPRESSION, YOUR IMAGE, AND MANY
IMPORTANT PERSONALITY TRAITS. THE
MOON, ALTHOUGH MERELY THE EARTH'S
SATELLITE, IS ASTRONOMICALLY THE
SECOND MOST IMPORTANT BODY IN THE
SOLAR SYSTEM. FROM THE SIGN THAT IT
WAS IN AT YOUR BIRTH, IT INFLUENCES HOW
YOU REACT TO SITUATIONS, YOUR
EMOTIONAL LEVEL, AND, TO A CERTAIN
EXTENT, WHAT YOU HAVE INHERITED FROM
YOUR PARENTS AND ANCESTORS. HAVING
FOUND YOUR MOON SIGN IN THE SIMPLE
TABLES ON PAGES 56 TO 59, TURN TO THE
RELEVANT PAGES AND TAKE A STEP
FORWARD IN YOUR OWN SELF-KNOWLEDGE.

THE MOON IN
ARIES

YOUR ARIEN MOON WILL HEIGHTEN YOUR EMOTIONS AND ENHANCE
YOUR NATURALLY RAPID GEMINIAN REACTIONS.
IMPATIENCE AND RESTLESSNESS COULD LEAD YOU TO MAKE
CARELESS MISTAKES ON IMPORTANT PROJECTS.

Sun sign Geminians are always alert, and your Arien Moon will speed up your already very swift reactions to situations, making you, in this respect, exceptionally Geminian. You will be extremely quick to answer back, and you always have an incisive, particularly slick response when challenged. Even more than most people of your Sun sign, you will love argument and debate.

Self-expression

You will always be in a hurry, but be careful: Undue haste could cause you problems. Also make sure that a quick response is not a selfish response.

Fire and air blend well, so your fiery Moon will help you not only to express your emotions freely, but also to feel far less anxious about them. Your characteristic Geminian versatility is often driven by a marvelous enthusiasm. But, as you know, you tend to get bored rather

easily, and your Arien Moon will exacerbate this tendency. You must learn to keep it under control. Otherwise you will waste a great deal of energy on false starts.

Romance

You are more passionate than many Geminians, and tend to fall in love very quickly and easily. Although you may be familiar with the Geminian tendency to duality, this will be less characteristic of your personality. This does not mean that, over your lifetime, you are likely to have fewer partners than other Sun sign Geminians; only that a certain singularity of purpose is likely to deter you from having more than one lover at a time.

Your well-being

The Arien body area is the head, and there is a chance that you often bumped it when you were a

The Moon in Aries

youngster. This was because your instinctive hastiness, stemming from your Arien Moon, made you accident-prone. This could still be the case, and your hands and arms may get easily bruised, cut, or burned.

Planning ahead

You will not be particularly unhappy if you are presented with the opportunity to make money quickly. However, you should be careful when offered any kind of risky get-rich-quick scheme. You will probably do much better to encourage your instinct for investments that can be completely controlled.

Parenthood

You will be a very lively parent and will not find it difficult to keep up with, or indeed ahead of, your children's interests. You should have fun with your family, and they will enjoy your youthful, energetic approach toward them.

THE MOON IN
TAURUS

ALLOW THE STABILITY AND INNER CALM OF YOUR TAUREAN MOON
TO STEADY GEMINIAN IMPATIENCE AND RESTLESSNESS. IF
YOU THINK IDEAS THROUGH CAREFULLY, YOU WILL MAKE THE
MOST OF YOUR TREMENDOUS CAPABILITIES.

Your Taurean Moon will be very helpful in controlling your Geminian tendency to be a little reckless and superficial. It will stabilize your reactions and support them with a great deal of practical common sense. While it may slow down certain aspects of your behavior, it will add depth, kindness, and a warm sympathy to your dealings with other people.

Self-expression
You will be less inclined than many Geminians to talk about things that you are unsure of, and more ready to listen to others and empathize with them. Not only will you have more time for other people, but you will also be willing to use that time at a reasonable pace, without the haste and flurry of many Geminians.

Emotional and financial security may be far more important to you than you care to admit. You may need to consider this carefully when, for instance, you are choosing a career or thinking about changing your job.

Romance
It could be that your Moon sign will make you far less flirtatious and less likely to enjoy more than one partner at a time than is typical of your Sun sign. Your emotions are warmed and heightened by your Moon; you will trust them and will make an especially sensual lover. Take care, however, that you do not succumb to possessiveness, the worst Taurean fault. Some freedom is desirable for both you and your partner.

Your well-being
The Taurean body area covers the neck and throat. To a certain extent, these will be vulnerable, especially if you have been giving a speech or a lecture, or spiritedly arguing with friends. You may even lose your voice.

The Moon in Taurus

Needless to say, for you a cold will start with a sore throat. If this happens, do all you can to keep the cold from spreading to your lungs.

Planning ahead
You have a practical attitude toward finance and investment. Money is far less likely to burn a hole in your pocket than it is with most other Sun sign Geminians. You probably have a flair for selling and a strong instinct for business. You will invest wisely and, if you spurn any Geminian

attraction toward quick financial growth, you will make your money work well for you.

Parenthood
You will work hard for your children, giving them a secure home, and encouraging mind-stretching interests and excursions in free time. While you are able to understand their enthusiasms and opinions, you can be quite strict at times. This is actually something that they will appreciate when they are older.

THE MOON IN
GEMINI

WITH BOTH THE SUN AND THE MOON IN GEMINI AT THE
TIME OF YOUR BIRTH, YOU WERE BORN AT THE TIME OF
THE NEW MOON. GEMINI IS AN AIR SIGN, SO YOU ARE VERY
MUCH AN "AIR" PERSON – A DOUBLE GEMINI.

Reading a list of the characteristics of your very lively Geminian Sun sign, you will probably realize that a great many of them apply to you. On average, out of 20 personality traits attributed to a sign, most people recognize 11 or 12. For you the average will be considerably higher, since both the Sun and the Moon were in Gemini when you were born.

Self-expression
Your Sun and Moon combination make you eternally youthful and an excellent communicator. You will be forever talking and voicing your opinions and will have an instinctive urge to communicate with others. Of course, being so highly motivated in this way has its complications. Do you always give yourself time to think?

Superficiality, one of the more serious Geminian faults, could be a major stumbling block for you. Counter it not by suppressing your natural versatility, but by aiming to acquire a little more knowledge about the subjects you find interesting.

You could be very mistrustful about your feelings. But make sure that you do not rationalize your emotions out of existence, or suppress them so they are never freely expressed.

Romance
Geminian duality may well have an effect upon your love life. You could end up having two partners, both of whom you love, for quite different reasons. This can obviously cause complications and, while your Geminian ability to talk yourself out of difficult situations will certainly be useful, why treat anyone unfairly?

Your well-being
The comments concerning Geminian health (see pages 22 – 23) particularly apply to you. In addition, you may be exceptionally vulnerable to anxiety

The Moon in Gemini

and stress. It will be a very good idea for you to learn a relaxation technique such as yoga. This will help you to develop an inner calm – something that you may well need.

Planning ahead

Your attitude toward money may not be terribly sound. You will probably want to accumulate large amounts of it quickly, just so you can spend it. In fact, your general cleverness could actually lead to you being rather too clever in this area. Ensure that you do not invent money-making schemes that could end up collapsing like a house of cards.

Parenthood

You are among the most lively and forward-looking of all parents. In fact, you may even be ahead of your children's ideas and opinions. They will probably learn from you, but try to be consistent – and not too critical. As a double Gemini, both these tendencies could sometimes be a source of difficulty.

THE MOON IN
CANCER

YOU HAVE A WARM, CARING QUALITY THAT IS UNCOMMON AMONG
SUN SIGN GEMINIANS. BUT YOU COULD BE A COMPULSIVE,
EVEN OBSESSIVE, WORRIER. TO COUNTER THIS TENDENCY, DEVELOP
YOUR GEMINIAN LOGIC AND SKEPTICISM.

Because the Moon rules Cancer, its influence from that sign is very powerful. While it will affect your responses to situations, it will also have a more general effect on your personality. It is likely to make you a very caring, protective, and sympathetic person.

Self-expression

You are sensitive, and could well suffer from rapid mood swings. While you are unlikely to become quiet or morose, you will sometimes shift between feeling very positive and extroverted, and being less confident and self-expressive. Your Geminian Sun will, however, see to it that you are always able to express your emotions verbally.

You have a very powerful imagination, and should use it both positively and creatively, perhaps through writing or craftwork. But do not let your imagination work overtime in negative ways, since you are far more prone to worry than most people of your Sun sign. It is in this sphere of your life that Geminian logic must come to your aid.

Romance

Your emotional resources demand positive expression through a meaningful relationship. This will involve a partner with whom you have an excellent rapport – especially sexually. Beware of the Geminian tendency to always question your emotions. All Geminians must accept that they have a tendency to rationalize their feelings out of existence, and work against that.

Your well-being

The Cancerian body area covers the chest and the breasts, so a vulnerability to Geminian breathing problems and to bronchitis is increased. If they linger, consult your

The Moon in Cancer

doctor. The digestive system is also Cancerian: Be careful what you eat. You could suffer from digestive problems, especially when you are at all worried. Resist the instinctive tendency to worry. Counter the impulse with Geminian logic.

Planning ahead

Your intuition can help you in relation to finance. You may well have a sound business sense, and you could make a lot of money – perhaps by building a collection of unusual articles or antiques. (Do you find it difficult to throw anything away?) On the other hand if you really feel that a certain investment would be good, rely on your intuition.

Parenthood

You will be very eager to have your own home and children, and could well be somewhat overprotective toward them. Take care not to create a claustrophobic atmosphere, and be very careful not to attempt to cling to your children. Because you have a nostalgic streak, you may not be as forward-looking as most Geminians. At times, this could widen the generation gap.

THE MOON IN
LEO

GEMINIANS ARE THE NATURAL COMMUNICATORS OF THE ZODIAC.
COMBINE THIS QUALITY WITH LEO CREATIVITY, AND YOU
COULD WELL HAVE LITERARY POTENTIAL. YOU WILL ALWAYS THINK
BIG, AND HAVE A WARM HEART.

Here is a vibrant, positive combination of Gemini, an air sign, and Leo, a fire sign. Just as air fans and feeds fire, your fiery Moon sign fans and feeds the intellectual approach of your Sun sign. It allows you both more emotion than the average Geminian, and the passion with which to express it.

Self-expression

Anyone with a Leo emphasis to their personality has a creative streak, and you may well have a great urge to express yourself imaginatively and creatively, perhaps through writing or painting. You need a creative hobby of some kind, although it need not be one directly related to the fine arts.

You could tend to be more fixed in your opinions than many Geminians. This may not be altogether a bad thing; it will add stability to your character and help to mitigate any Geminian superficiality. You will tend to organize your thoughts and to consider your conclusions. Make sure that you do not become dogmatic.

Romance

You make a wonderful lover, far more passionate than many people of your Sun sign are. You will lavish not only love and affection on your partner, but also a very varied and energetic form of sexual expression.

Elegance and comfort will be as important in this sphere of your life as in every other, and you will spend a lot of money in order to ensure it for you and your partner.

Your well-being

The Leo body areas are the spine and heart, and it is very important that you sit properly, especially if you spend hours at an office desk. A well-designed chair will be especially helpful to you. Make time to regularly exercise your spine. Equally, while

The Moon in Leo

you are no more prone to heart attacks than anyone else, it is obvious that you should exercise to keep that vital organ in good working order. You are easily bored with exercise, so vary your routine as much as possible. If you jog, cover a different route each day; alternatively, a health club, with all its varied activities, should keep you happy.

Planning ahead
Because of a liking for luxury and real quality, you probably need to make a lot of money. But you also need inner fulfillment from your work; if you do not get it you will tend to flit from one job to the next, and so never have enough cash to live in the style to which you aspire. You should be fairly good at investing.

Parenthood
You will want to encourage your children, urging them to enjoy a great variety of interests. You will take them on delightful and memorable outings, for example, to museums and theaters. They will be grateful for this and will enjoy your company as much as you enjoy theirs. However, try not to boss them around too much.

THE MOON IN
VIRGO

GEMINI AND VIRGO ARE BOTH RULED BY MERCURY, SO THERE
IS A NATURAL EMPATHY BETWEEN THE TWO
SIGNS. YOUR MIND IS VERY SHARP AND ANALYTICAL, BUT
YOU EXPRESS YOUR EMOTIONS FREELY.

Here is an example of a positive air sign (Gemini) combining with a negative earth sign (Virgo). Both signs are, however, of the mutable quality, and also share Mercury as their ruling planet.

Self-expression

You are extroverted, and a wonderful communicator. Your instincts are very practical and, although you could well be overly talkative, you will make sure of your facts before expressing your opinion. You can be extremely critical, so make an effort to express your views constructively.

Do not dither or start too many jobs at the same time. You may need to develop better organizational skills.

Romance

Virgoan modesty and a rather low emotional level, together with Geminian shyness about the expression of emotion, may lead you to mistrust your feelings and conceal them. If you lack confidence, you might benefit from counseling.

Your well-being

The Virgoan body area is the stomach, and in some cases this can become vulnerable, especially when you are worried. To overcome this, use your rational, logical approach to problems, instead of your intuition.

You need a high-fiber diet to keep your bowels in good order; many people with a strong Virgoan influence are successful on a vegetarian diet. All health foods can be beneficial to you, and you might consider investigating homeopathy and complementary medicine. With your Sun and Moon combination, you should respond very positively to them. Try to control restlessness and to develop a sense of inner peace: you will benefit from yoga or a similar discipline. If you allow tension to get

The Moon in Virgo

the better of you, there is a chance that you could become prone to migraines, which is a Virgoan ailment.

Planning ahead
Your Virgoan Moon will encourage you to be more careful with money than most Sun sign Geminians. Respond to the influence of your Moon sign, and keep a careful count of your money before you succumb to any Geminian frivolity. Mercury is the planet of trade and commerce, and

you are therefore in a good position to obtain excellent returns for any outlay. Just think carefully, critically, and practically when you invest.

Parenthood
You will be an energetic, hardworking parent, but do not allow yourself to be ruled by chores. Let your children persuade you to take them out. You will argue and discuss things with them in the best possible way, so avoid nagging them.

THE MOON IN
LIBRA

BOTH GEMINI AND LIBRA ARE AIR SIGNS, INCLINING THEIR
SUBJECTS TO BE UNDERSTANDING AND RATIONAL.
YOU MAY BE COMMUNICATIVE, BUT YOU COULD HAVE DEEP
EMOTIONS THAT ARE STILL WAITING TO BE EXPRESSED.

Your Geminian intellect is spiced with Libran charm, delicacy of approach, and love of balance, harmony, and comfort.

Self-expression
You are wonderfully diplomatic in a natural, instinctive way. Social intercourse is very important to you, and you probably show an automatic interest in everyone that you meet. No doubt you have a very wide circle of friends, among whom you give the impression that you know a lot about almost everything.

Geminian logic can be weakened by Libran indecisiveness. Do not be evasive or push decisions onto other people; be self-critical and you will manage to overcome the tendency.

Romance
While Libra makes you respond immediately both to the idea of romance and to romantic situations, it

may be that you tend to fall in love with love itself. In spite of a longing for romance, Libra is not really a very deeply emotional sign – and neither is Gemini. Do not let an idea be a substitute for reality.

Your well-being
You may be somewhat prone to headaches. These could relate to your kidneys – which are the Libran organ and therefore slightly vulnerable. You could, perhaps, suffer from some pain in the lumbar region of your back. This, too, may be attributable to your Libran Moon. In general make sure that you sit upright when working at a table or a desk.

Exercise will probably bore you even more than most Geminians. To keep in shape, devise a system of rewards for yourself – for example, a relaxed half hour in a sauna or steam bath, or a talk with friends at the salad bar after your workout. But be careful:

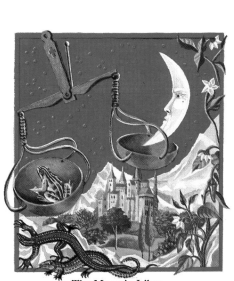

The Moon in Libra

Your Libran Moon may also give you more of a sweet tooth than most Geminians, and your waistline could suffer if you make that reward a slice of chocolate cake. The normally quick Geminian metabolism may, of course, be of some assistance here.

Planning ahead

Librans enjoy comfort and luxury. Beautiful clothes and expensive beauty products and treatments are therefore likely to cost you a lot of money. You will probably do well to take sound financial advice before investing, since you could instinctively fall for a whim that sounds good or glamorous, and end up losing in the long run.

Parenthood

You will be a kind, sympathetic parent, but might tend to bribe your children for the sake of peace and quiet. If you are too easy with them, they will soon learn to twist you around their little fingers. Use your Geminian astuteness.

THE MOON IN
SCORPIO

YOUR BASIC INSTINCTS ARE VERY PASSIONATE, AND YOU ARE
PARTICULARLY INTUITIVE. DO NOT ALLOW GEMINIAN
LOGIC TO SUPPRESS THESE TRAITS. YOUR INQUIRING MIND MAY LEAD
YOU TO BE SOMETHING OF A DETECTIVE.

A combination of Sun and Moon signs that is this dynamic is apt to make you a Geminian with a big difference. Your Scorpio Moon gives you a powerful emotional force that demands much positive expression if you are to achieve inner fulfillment.

Self-expression
If your general restlessness is not to be coupled with discontent and frustration, you must find work that is very satisfying. Go all out to achieve your aims, allowing your Geminian versatility full rein.

Unlike many Sun sign Geminians, you are not superficial; you need to get to the root of every problem.

Romance
Your emotional resources are so strong that you are unlikely to fall into the trap of letting them be dominated by your Geminian logic. Just as you need to be fulfilled in your career, so you

need fulfillment in an emotional relationship. Sexual satisfaction is of above-average importance to you, and you probably demand a great deal from partners in this respect. It is important that they respond positively, perceiving your needs and being sympathetic to them. Geminians like to experiment, and this, too, is vital for you.

Your well-being
The Scorpio body area is the genitals, and regular clinical checkups in this region are always a good idea. Safe sex is another obvious precaution that both sexes should consider.

Should a mysterious illness strike you down, it may be that, contrary to the instinct of most Geminians, you are denying a problem.

Scorpios love rich food and fine wine, and while many have a wiry build, if by chance you are thick-set or have a slower metabolism than

The Moon in Scorpio

average, you could suffer from obesity and a sluggish system. Try not to get bored with exercise – perhaps taking up judo or karate would be the solution. All kinds of sports can be enjoyable if approached correctly.

Planning ahead

Your shrewdness, intelligence, and cunning, enhanced by the influence of Gemini and Scorpio, will no doubt help you to make money, so act without hesitation. Your bank balance should grow steadily, even if you occasionally go wild on a case of wine or other expensive treats.

Parenthood

As a parent, you may be stricter than you realize, and could easily overreact to any misdemeanors. On the whole, however, your Geminian Sun keeps you very youthful and in no way pedantic. You should enjoy your role as parent and have time for fun with your children.

THE MOON IN
SAGITTARIUS

AS GEMINI AND SAGITTARIUS ARE POLAR OR OPPOSITE ZODIAC
SIGNS, YOU WERE BORN UNDER A FULL MOON. YOU MAY
FIND IT HARD TO CONTROL AN INHERENT RESTLESSNESS. BE
VERSATILE, BUT DEVELOP CONSISTENCY OF EFFORT.

Each of us is, in one way or another, liable to express certain attributes of our polar, or opposite, Zodiac signs. For Geminians, the polar sign is Sagittarius, and as the Moon was in that sign when you were born, the polarity is powerfully emphasized. A great deal of sympathy and empathy exists between Gemini and Sagittarius: both are positive, mutable signs, and are complementary air and fire signs.

Self-expression

Your Geminian communicative ability is emphasized by an instinct that will help you get your ideas across to others with tremendous enthusiasm. Your natural optimism is very infectious, and you will easily win others around to your point of view.

Your life needs challenge, but do not start looking for alternatives just for the sake of it. Sagittarius, like Gemini, gives its subjects a versatility

that needs to be expressed, but to get the best effect from it, you need to always be consistent in what you do. The worst Sagittarian fault is restlessness, and those, like yourself, who are born under a Full Moon are especially prone to it.

Romance

You make the liveliest of lovers, and possess a fiery passion. You need partners who, if anything, are ahead of you in their eagerness to experiment with, and enjoy, a physical relationship. It is, however, equally important that your partners have excellent minds; otherwise, you will be unlikely to develop any true and lasting friendship with them.

Your well-being

The Sagittarian body area covers the hips and thighs, and women with this sign emphasized tend to put on weight in these areas. You may well

The Moon in Sagittarius

enjoy rather heavier food than other
Sun sign Geminians, and this could
make matters worse. The liver is the
Sagittarian organ, so hangovers may
be something of a problem for you.
Like all Geminians and Sagittarians,
you need plenty of variety in anything
that you do, to combat boredom.

Planning ahead

It is probably true to say that while,
like everyone, you generally need
money, it is usually there when you
want it. You may not be very
interested in investments, and could
well have something of a gambling

streak, which you should be wary of.
If you enjoy rather risky deals or
gambling on the stockmarket, do not
invest more money than you know
you can afford to lose.

Parenthood

Your children will find your natural
enthusiasm for life infectious.
Bringing them up should not prove to
be too much of a worry or problem,
since you are so young at heart
yourself. You are also a natural
teacher, and will keep their minds
usefully occupied. For you, the
generation gap simply does not exist.

THE MOON IN
CAPRICORN

GEMINI, WHICH IS AN AIR SIGN, IS NOT PARTICULARLY COMPATIBLE
WITH CAPRICORN, AN EARTH SIGN. THE DIFFERENT
CHARACTERISTICS THAT YOUR MOON SIGN ADDS TO YOUR
PERSONALITY ARE STILL VERY INTERESTING.

Your natural instincts tell you to be practical, aspiring, and ambitious. But to develop single-minded purpose may prove difficult for a versatile Sun sign Geminian. Try to compromise where and when you can.

Self-expression
You are among the most practical members of your Sun sign group, and need a secure base upon which to build your life. Gemini is a take-charge sign, and the influence of your Moon will be to urge you on.

Aspiring with determination, you know that you will achieve the ambition on which you have set your sights. That ambition is, however, just as likely to center on a contented family with an ideal home as on some professional aspiration.

You may be a little more susceptible to worry than other Sun sign Geminians. Should this lead to bouts of despondency, let your

Geminian logic and optimism take control and rationalize any problems that you are having.

Romance
Your Moon sign does not increase your ability to express your emotions freely. While you are friendly and sociable, you may tend to distance yourself from your true feelings and, in doing so, suppress them.

You need a partner who is as ambitious as you are and capable of being a good friend within any emotional relationship. Sex may not be the main reason why you want to deepen a relationship, but sexual fulfillment is as necessary for you as it is for anyone else.

Your well-being
The Capricornian body area covers the knees and shins, which are therefore vulnerable. Fortunately, Geminians like to keep moving, so

The Moon in Capricorn

Capricornian stiffness of the joints should not be too much of a problem. The teeth are also ruled by Capricorn, so regular dental checkups are of paramount importance for you.

Planning ahead
As far as finances are concerned, your instinct is to save money and to be very careful with it. But when your Geminian Sun takes over, you will feel that you want to enjoy the fruits of your hard-earned cash. Consequently, you could be faced with something of a conflict. However, you should have a skill for budgeting and investment.

Parenthood
You may give the impression that you are a strict and rigid parent, but with your Capricornian sense of humor, your children will know that this is not entirely the case. If you make sure that you have time to enjoy their company and listen to their opinions, the generation gap should not be much of a problem for you.

THE MOON IN
AQUARIUS

MODERN, FORWARD-LOOKING GEMINIANS WITH A TRENDY IMAGE
WILL USE AN AQUARIAN URGE FOR GLAMOUR AND ORIGINALITY
TO GREAT EFFECT. DO NOT LET YOUR NEED FOR INDEPENDENCE
EXCLUDE MEANINGFUL EMOTIONAL RELATIONSHIPS.

You have an extremely interesting combination of intellectually inclined signs, both of which are of the air element. You are original and very logical, if slightly unpredictable.

Self-expression
You are among the most independent of Geminians, and many of you will build a lifestyle that could well have some unique features to it.

Aquarius is a sign of the fixed quality, so you may well have to bring your Geminian Sun into play if you have a tendency to be stubborn.

While Gemini has the reputation of being the most youthful of signs, Aquarius is high on the list of the most glamorous ones. Neither sign is very emotional. There is, in fact, a rather distant quality to many Aquarians. They tend to give the impression that while you may look at and admire them, you should also keep your distance.

Romance
It is very important for both you and your partner to recognize the fact that you will always need a considerable measure of independence. Perhaps contrarily, your Moon makes you a great romantic. You will no doubt love all the trimmings of romance, for example, bouquets of flowers, wonderful candle-lit dinners, and Valentine cards. Sexual fulfillment must, for you, be colored with romance – the atmosphere has to be just right. It should not be too difficult for you to persuade your partners to go along with this.

Your well-being
The Aquarian body area covers the ankles. If you like wearing high-heeled shoes, be careful. Aquarius also rules the circulation and, while most people with this sign emphasized in their birthcharts enjoy cold weather, their circulation is not

The Moon in Aquarius

always good. Perhaps you enjoy winter sports: these will be good for you, provided that you keep warm.

Planning ahead
You may not be very good with money. Gemini likes to keep up to date, especially in image, and Aquarius is easily attracted to rather glitzy, ephemeral things. You might, for example, want to back a theater show, but no quicker way of losing money has yet been invented.

Always talk potential investments over with a sound financial adviser. This will teach you how to handle your finances, and you will not have to learn the hard way.

Parenthood
You will be a typically forward-looking Geminian parent. You will sympathize with your children when they are upset, but sometimes in a too-adult way, discussing their problems when they need a cuddle.

THE MOON IN
PISCES

THE AIR ELEMENT OF GEMINI CAN CLASH WITH THE EMOTIONAL
CONTENT OF A PISCEAN WATER SIGN. ALLOW YOUR
EMOTION TO FLOW, PERHAPS THROUGH ARTISTIC APPRECIATION
OR EXPRESSION; DO NOT RATIONALIZE IT AWAY.

Although there is a clash of elements in this combination – Gemini is air and Pisces, water – both the Sun and the Moon work very well for you. On the whole, Pisces is a creative sign, and those in whose charts it is emphasized will long for some kind of creative expression.

Self-expression

You are, by nature, very versatile and probably like to have many tasks at hand at the same time. For all Geminians, developing consistency of effort and learning to finish all the tasks undertaken, is extremely important. If you do not do this, inner fulfillment will evade you.

You are likely to be very emotional. Because this trait is linked to your deepest instinctive level, you will tend to overrationalize a situation once you are aware that you are reacting emotionally to it. You will question yourself about your emotions, and may mistrust and even be inclined to suppress them. Be aware that by giving your emotions full rein, you will gain in the long run.

Romance

You make a delightful lover and are more caring of your partners – perhaps also more easily hurt, than many Geminians. Remember that Piscean and Geminian duality, plus a touch of deceit, could make for complications in your emotional life. Sexually, you enjoy variety as well as passion. But you do need to have a solid intellectual rapport and shared interests with any partners.

Your well-being

The Piscean body area is the feet, and they will be very vulnerable to blisters, corns, and cuts.

Even more than most Geminians, you are likely to worry or be apprehensive. If this is the case, let

The Moon in Pisces

your Geminian rationality take over. The best kind of exercise for you is likely to be swimming or any kind of dancing or skating.

Planning ahead

Financially, you should obtain professional advice regarding investment. As you can be a very soft touch indeed, you would be well advised not to lend money.

Parenthood

You will be a warm and loving parent, although you may sometimes have a tendency to spoil your children. You will also be very good at encouraging their interests, sometimes even getting yourself involved in things you never thought could possibly interest you. Your children will, of course, greatly appreciate this, and there is always the chance that they might even become hooked on a hobby or interest that particularly fascinates you.

The one thing that you should beware of is acting evasively toward them. It is always important for children to know exactly where they stand with their parents. In your case, the generation gap should not exist.

MOON CHARTS

REFER TO THE FOLLOWING TABLES TO DISCOVER YOUR MOON SIGN.
THE PRECEDING PAGES WILL TELL YOU ABOUT ITS QUALITIES.

By referring to the charts on pages 57, 58 and 59 locate the Zodiacal glyph for the month of the year in which you were born. Using the Moon table on this page, find the number opposite the day you were born that month. Then, starting from the glyph you found first, count off that number using the list of Zodiacal glyphs (below, right). You may have to count to Pisces and continue with Aries. For example, if you were born on May 21, 1991, first you need to find the Moon sign on the chart on page 59. Look down the chart to May; the glyph is

Sagittarius (♐). Then consult the Moon table for the 21st. It tells you to add nine glyphs. Starting from Sagittarius, count down nine, and you find your Moon sign is Virgo (♍).

Note that because the Moon moves so quickly, it is beyond the scope of this little book to provide a detailed chart of its positions. For more detailed horoscopes, you will need to consult an astrologer, but if you feel that this chart gives a result that does not seem to apply to you, read the pages for the signs either before or after the one indicated; one of the three will apply.

MOON TABLE

DAYS OF THE MONTH AND NUMBER OF
SIGNS THAT SHOULD BE ADDED

DAY	ADD	DAY	ADD	DAY	ADD	DAY	ADD
1	0	9	4	17	7	25	11
2	1	10	4	18	8	26	11
3	1	11	5	19	8	27	12
4	1	12	5	20	9	28	12
5	2	13	5	21	9	29	1
6	2	14	6	22	10	30	1
7	3	15	6	23	10	31	2
8	3	16	7	24	10		

ZODIACAL GLYPHS

♈	Aries
♉	Taurus
♊	Gemini
♋	Cancer
♌	Leo
♍	Virgo
♎	Libra
♏	Scorpio
♐	Sagittarius
♑	Capricorn
♒	Aquarius
♓	Pisces

	1923	1924	1925	1926	1927	1928	1929	1930	1931	1932	1933	1934	1935
JAN	♊	♏	♈	♌	♐	♈	♍	♑	♉	♎	♓	♋	♏
FEB	♌	♐	♉	♍	♑	♊	♏	♓	♋	♐	♈	♌	♑
MAR	♌	♑	♉	♍	♒	♋	♏	♓	♋	♐	♉	♍	♑
APR	♎	♓	♋	♏	♈	♍	♑	♉	♍	♒	♊	♎	♓
MAY	♏	♈	♌	♐	♉	♎	♒	♊	♎	♓	♋	♐	♈
JUN	♑	♉	♍	♒	♋	♏	♓	♌	♐	♉	♍	♑	♊
JUL	♒	♋	♏	♓	♌	♐	♈	♍	♑	♊	♎	♓	♋
AUG	♈	♌	♐	♉	♍	♒	♊	♏	♓	♋	♐	♈	♌
SEP	♉	♎	♒	♋	♏	♓	♌	♐	♈	♍	♑	♊	♎
OCT	♊	♏	♓	♌	♐	♉	♍	♑	♉	♎	♓	♋	♏
NOV	♌	♑	♉	♍	♑	♊	♏	♓	♋	♐	♈	♌	♑
DEC	♍	♒	♊	♎	♓	♌	♐	♈	♌	♑	♉	♍	♒

	1936	1937	1938	1939	1940	1941	1942	1943	1944	1945	1946	1947	1948
JAN	♈	♌	♑	♉	♍	♒	♊	♎	♓	♌	♐	♈	♍
FEB	♉	♎	♒	♊	♏	♈	♌	♐	♉	♍	♑	♊	♎
MAR	♊	♎	♒	♋	♐	♈	♌	♐	♉	♎	♒	♊	♏
APR	♌	♐	♈	♌	♑	♉	♎	♒	♋	♏	♓	♌	♑
MAY	♍	♑	♉	♎	♒	♊	♏	♓	♌	♐	♉	♍	♒
JUN	♎	♒	♋	♏	♈	♌	♑	♉	♎	♒	♊	♏	♓
JUL	♏	♈	♌	♑	♉	♍	♒	♊	♏	♓	♌	♐	♈
AUG	♑	♉	♎	♒	♋	♏	♈	♌	♐	♉	♍	♑	♊
SEP	♓	♋	♏	♈	♌	♑	♉	♍	♒	♋	♏	♓	♌
OCT	♈	♌	♑	♉	♎	♒	♊	♎	♓	♌	♐	♈	♍
NOV	♊	♎	♒	♊	♏	♈	♌	♐	♉	♍	♑	♊	♏
DEC	♋	♏	♓	♌	♑	♉	♍	♑	♊	♎	♒	♋	♐

	1949	1950	1951	1952	1953	1954	1955	1956	1957	1958	1959	1960	1961
JAN	♑	♊	♎	♓	♋	♏	♈	♌	♑	♉	♍	♒	♋
FEB	♓	♋	♐	♈	♍	♑	♉	♎	♒	♊	♏	♈	♌
MAR	♓	♋	♐	♉	♍	♑	♊	♏	♓	♋	♏	♈	♌
APR	♉	♍	♒	♊	♎	♓	♋	♐	♈	♌	♑	♊	♎
MAY	♊	♎	♓	♋	♐	♈	♍	♑	♉	♎	♒	♋	♏
JUN	♌	♐	♈	♍	♑	♊	♎	♓	♋	♐	♈	♌	♑
JUL	♍	♑	♊	♎	♓	♋	♏	♈	♌	♑	♉	♍	♒
AUG	♏	♓	♋	♐	♈	♍	♑	♉	♎	♒	♊	♏	♈
SEP	♐	♈	♍	♑	♊	♎	♒	♋	♐	♈	♌	♑	♊
OCT	♑	♊	♎	♓	♋	♏	♓	♌	♑	♉	♍	♒	♋
NOV	♓	♋	♏	♈	♍	♑	♉	♎	♒	♊	♏	♈	♌
DEC	♈	♌	♑	♊	♎	♒	♊	♏	♓	♌	♐	♉	♍

	1962	1963	1964	1965	1966	1967	1968	1969	1970	1971	1972	1973	1974
JAN	♏	♓	♌	♐	♈	♍	♑	♊	♎	♒	♋	♐	♈
FEB	♐	♉	♍	♒	♊	♏	♓	♋	♏	♈	♍	♑	♉
MAR	♐	♉	♎	♒	♊	♏	♈	♌	♐	♉	♍	♑	♊
APR	♒	♋	♏	♈	♌	♑	♉	♍	♒	♊	♍	♓	♋
MAY	♓	♌	♐	♉	♍	♒	♊	♎	♓	♌	♐	♈	♍
JUN	♉	♎	♒	♊	♏	♓	♌	♐	♉	♍	♑	♊	♎
JUL	♊	♏	♓	♌	♐	♈	♍	♑	♊	♎	♓	♋	♐
AUG	♌	♐	♉	♎	♒	♊	♏	♓	♋	♏	♈	♍	♑
SEP	♍	♒	♋	♏	♓	♋	♐	♉	♍	♑	♊	♎	♓
OCT	♏	♓	♌	♐	♈	♍	♒	♊	♎	♒	♋	♐	♈
NOV	♐	♉	♎	♒	♊	♎	♓	♋	♐	♈	♍	♑	♉
DEC	♑	♊	♏	♓	♋	♐	♈	♌	♑	♉	♎	♒	♊

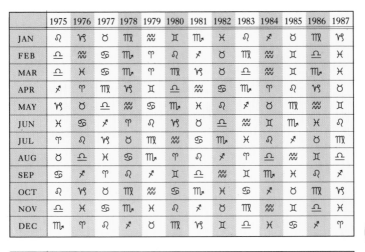

	1975	1976	1977	1978	1979	1980	1981	1982	1983	1984	1985	1986	1987
JAN	♌	♑	♉	♍	♒	♊	♏	♓	♌	♐	♉	♍	♑
FEB	♎	♒	♋	♏	♈	♌	♐	♉	♍	♒	♊	♎	♓
MAR	♎	♓	♋	♏	♈	♍	♑	♉	♎	♒	♊	♏	♓
APR	♐	♈	♍	♑	♊	♎	♒	♋	♏	♈	♌	♑	♉
MAY	♑	♉	♎	♒	♋	♏	♓	♌	♐	♉	♍	♒	♊
JUN	♓	♋	♐	♈	♌	♑	♉	♎	♒	♊	♏	♓	♌
JUL	♈	♌	♑	♉	♍	♒	♋	♏	♓	♌	♐	♉	♍
AUG	♉	♎	♓	♋	♏	♈	♌	♐	♈	♎	♒	♊	♎
SEP	♋	♐	♈	♌	♐	♊	♎	♒	♊	♏	♓	♌	♐
OCT	♌	♑	♉	♍	♒	♋	♏	♓	♋	♐	♉	♍	♑
NOV	♎	♓	♋	♏	♓	♌	♐	♉	♍	♒	♊	♎	♓
DEC	♏	♈	♌	♐	♉	♍	♑	♊	♎	♓	♋	♐	♈

	1988	1989	1990	1991	1992	1993	1994	1995	1996	1997	1998	1999	2000
JAN	♊	♎	♒	♋	♏	♈	♌	♑	♉	♎	♒	♊	♏
FEB	♋	♐	♈	♍	♑	♉	♎	♒	♋	♏	♈	♌	♐
MAR	♌	♐	♉	♍	♒	♊	♎	♓	♋	♏	♈	♌	♑
APR	♍	♒	♊	♏	♓	♋	♐	♈	♍	♑	♊	♎	♓
MAY	♏	♓	♌	♐	♈	♍	♑	♉	♎	♒	♋	♏	♈
JUN	♐	♉	♍	♑	♊	♎	♓	♋	♐	♈	♌	♑	♉
JUL	♑	♊	♎	♒	♋	♐	♈	♌	♑	♉	♎	♒	♋
AUG	♓	♌	♐	♈	♍	♑	♉	♎	♓	♋	♏	♓	♌
SEP	♉	♍	♑	♊	♏	♓	♋	♏	♈	♌	♑	♉	♎
OCT	♊	♎	♒	♋	♐	♈	♌	♑	♉	♎	♒	♊	♏
NOV	♌	♐	♈	♍	♑	♉	♎	♒	♋	♏	♈	♌	♑
DEC	♍	♑	♉	♎	♒	♋	♏	♈	♌	♐	♉	♍	♒

THE SOLAR SYSTEM

THE STARS, OTHER THAN THE SUN, PLAY NO PART IN THE SCIENCE
OF ASTROLOGY. ASTROLOGERS USE ONLY THE BODIES IN THE
SOLAR SYSTEM, EXCLUDING THE EARTH, TO CALCULATE HOW OUR
LIVES AND PERSONALITIES CHANGE.

Pluto
Pluto takes 246 years to travel around
the Sun. It affects our unconscious
instincts and urges, gives us strength
in difficulty, and perhaps emphasizes
any inherent cruel streak.

Neptune
Neptune stays in each sign for 14
years. At best it makes us sensitive
and imaginative; at worst it
encourages deceit and carelessness,
making us worry.

Uranus
The influence of Uranus can make us
friendly, kind, eccentric, inventive,
and unpredictable.

Saturn
In ancient times, Saturn was the most
distant known planet. Its influence
can limit our ambition and make us
either overly cautious (but practical),
or reliable and self-disciplined.

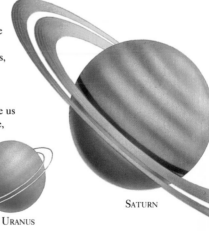

PLUTO

NEPTUNE

URANUS

SATURN

Jupiter

Jupiter encourages expansion, optimism, generosity, and breadth of vision. It can, however, also make us wasteful, extravagant, and conceited.

Mars

Much associated with energy, anger, violence, selfishness, and a strong sex drive, Mars also encourages decisiveness and leadership.

JUPITER

Earth

Every planet contributes to the environment of the Solar System, and a person born on Venus would no doubt be influenced by our own planet in some way.

The Moon

Although it is a satellite of the Earth, the Moon is known in astrology as a planet. It lies about 240,000 miles from the Earth and, astrologically, is second in importance to the Sun.

 MERCURY

THE MOON

 VENUS

EARTH

MARS

The Sun

The Sun, the only star used by astrologers, influences the way we present ourselves to the world – our image or personality, the "us" we show to other people.

Venus

The planet of love and partnership, Venus can emphasize all our best personal qualities. It may also encourage us to be lazy, impractical, and too dependent on other people.

Mercury

The planet closest to the Sun affects our intellect. It can make us inquisitive, versatile, argumentative, perceptive, and clever, but maybe also inconsistent, cynical, and sarcastic.